THE 100 BEST LOVE POEMS *of* ALL TIME

Also Edited by Leslie Pockell

The 100 Best Poems of All Time
The 13 Best Horror Stories of All Time

THE 100 BEST LOVE POEMS of ALL TIME

EDITED BY

LESLIE POCKELL

with **Adrienne Avila**
and **Katharine Rapkin**

DOUBLEDAY LARGE PRINT HOME LIBRARY EDITION

WARNER BOOKS

An AOL Time Warner Company

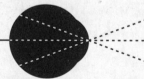

This Large Print Book carries the
Seal of Approval of N.A.V.H.

Contents

Introduction   xi

La Vita Nuova ∽ DANTE ALIGHIERI   1

Shall I Compare Thee to a Summer's Day? ∽
WILLIAM SHAKESPEARE   2

Shall I Compare Thee to a Summer's Day? ∽
HOWARD MOSS   4

Who Ever Loved ∽ CHRISTOPHER MARLOWE   5

from Paradise Lost (Book IV) ∽ JOHN MILTON   6

To Helen ∽ EDGAR ALLAN POE   8

A Red, Red Rose ∽ ROBERT BURNS   9

She Tells Her Love while Half Asleep ∽
ROBERT GRAVES   10

Last Night You Left Me and Slept ∽
RUMI   11

I Prithee Send Me Back My Heart ∽
SIR JOHN SUCKLING   12

I Carry Your Heart with Me ∽ E. E. CUMMINGS   14

The Avenue ∽ FRANCES CORNFORD   16

The Bargain ∽ SIR PHILIP SIDNEY   17

The Mirabeau Bridge ∽ GUILLAUME APOLLINAIRE   18

To the Bridge of Love ∽ JUAN RAMON JIMENEZ   20

She Walks in Beauty ∽ LORD BYRON   21

The Ragged Wood ∽ WILLIAM BUTLER YEATS   22

Night Thoughts ∽

    JOHANN WOLFGANG VON GOETHE   23

The Gardener ∽ RABINDRANATH TAGORE   24

To the Harbormaster ∽ FRANK O'HARA   26

To a Stranger ∽ WALT WHITMAN   28

True Love ∽ JUDITH VIORST   30

Love 20 Cents the First Quarter Mile ∽

    KENNETH FEARING   33

Jenny Kiss'd Me ∽ LEIGH HUNT   36

Juliet ∽ HILAIRE BELLOC   37

Song to Celia ∽ BEN JONSON   38

Your Catfish Friend ∽ RICHARD BRAUTIGAN   39

The Owl and the Pussy-Cat ∽ EDWARD LEAR   41

Love Song to Alex, 1979 ∽ MARGARET WALKER   43

When Sue Wears Red ∽ LANGSTON HUGHES   45

Those Who Love ∽ SARA TEASDALE   46

Reprise ∽ OGDEN NASH   47

One Word Is Too Often Profaned ∽

    PERCY BYSSHE SHELLEY   48

I Do Not Love You ∽ PABLO NERUDA   49

Gifts ∽ JULIANA HORATIA EWING   51

At Last ∽ ELIZABETH AKERS ALLEN   52

To Alice B. Toklas ∽ GERTRUDE STEIN   54

Valentine ∽ DONALD HALL   55

Love's Secret ∽ WILLIAM BLAKE   56

I Knew a Woman ∽ THEODORE ROETHKE   57

Love for a Hand ∽ KARL SHAPIRO   60

It Is the Third Watch ∽ ANONYMOUS   62

The Enchantment ∽ THOMAS OTWAY   63

The Silken Tent ∽ ROBERT FROST   64

Love Song ∽ WILLIAM CARLOS WILLIAMS   66

Wild Nights! ∽ EMILY DICKINSON   67

*She Comes Not When Noon Is on the
Roses* ∽ HERBERT TRENCH   68

Between Your Sheets ∽
LADY MARY WORTLEY MONTAGU   69

The Jewels ∽ CHARLES BAUDELAIRE   71

Song 5 to Lesbia ∽ CATULLUS
(GAIUS VALERIUS CATULLUS)   74

The Vine ∽ JAMES THOMSON   75

from The Song of Songs ∽ ANONYMOUS
(ATTRIBUTED TO KING SOLOMON)   76

Confession ∽ FRANTISEK HALAS   78

I Loved You ∽ ALEXANDER SERGEYEVICH PUSHKIN   79

from Merciless Beauty ∽ GEOFFREY CHAUCER   80

He Is More than a Hero ∽ SAPPHO   81

To His Mistress ∽ JOHN WILMOT,
EARL OF ROCHESTER   83

To Little or No Purpose ∽
SIR GEORGE ETHEREGE   84

Touch ∽ OCTAVIO PAZ   86

vii

Lady Love ∽ SAMUEL BECKETT 87

Love Poem ∽ GREGORY ORR 88

I Want to Breathe ∽ JAMES LAUGHLIN 89

A Statue of Eros ∽ ZENODOTOS 90

Come Quickly ∽ IZUMI SHIKIBU 91

Let Me Not to the Marriage of True Minds ∽

    WILLIAM SHAKESPEARE 92

Habitation ∽ MARGARET ATWOOD 93

September ∽ TED HUGHES 94

Love Letter ∽ SYLVIA PLATH 96

Marriage Morning ∽ ALFRED, LORD TENNYSON 98

To My Dear and Loving Husband ∽

    ANNE BRADSTREET 100

Fulfillment ∽ WILLIAM CAVENDISH 101

How Do I Love Thee? ∽

    ELIZABETH BARRETT BROWNING 103

Meeting at Night ∽ ROBERT BROWNING 105

Sonnet XXX ∽ EDNA ST. VINCENT MILLAY 106

Camomile Tea ∽ KATHERINE MANSFIELD 107

Decade ∽ AMY LOWELL 109

Wear Me ∽ ROBERT KOGAN 110

The Marriage ∽ YVOR WINTERS 111

Married Love ∽ TAO-SHENG 113

The River Merchant's Wife ∽ LI PO 114

To His Coy Mistress ∽ ANDREW MARVELL 117

Nothing Twice ∽ WISLAWA SZYMBORSKA 120

Strawberries ∽ EDWIN MORGAN 122

True Love ∽ ROBERT PENN WARREN 124

When I Was One-and-Twenty ∽
   A. E. HOUSMAN   *127*

Thunderstorm in Town ∽ THOMAS HARDY   *128*

On the Balcony ∽ D. H. LAWRENCE   *129*

Love Song ∽ RAINER MARIA RILKE   *131*

Moonlit Night ∽ TU FU   *133*

Sonnet of Sweet Complaint ∽
   FEDERICO GARCIA LORCA   *134*

Since There's No Help ∽ MICHAEL DRAYTON   *135*

Love Arm'd ∽ APHRA BEHN   *136*

The Lost Love ∽ WILLIAM WORDSWORTH   *138*

Echo ∽ CHRISTINA ROSSETTI   *139*

Reminiscence ∽ ANNE BRONTE   *141*

For Jane ∽ CHARLES BUKOWSKI   *143*

Funeral Blues ∽ W. H. AUDEN   *144*

Vino Tinto ∽ SANDRA CISNEROS   *146*

One Art ∽ ELIZABETH BISHOP   *147*

To Fanny Brawne ∽ JOHN KEATS   *149*

A Valediction Forbidding Mourning ∽
   JOHN DONNE   *150*

Index to Titles and Authors   *153*

Index to First Lines   *161*

Acknowledgments   *167*

Introduction

As with this book's predecessor, *The 100 Best Poems of All Time,* our primary objective in assembling these works has been to provide a small, easily portable volume that would contain the essential works that most readers would expect to find in a book of this kind, along with a few discoveries. Love poetry down the years seems to have been written along a spectrum ranging from idealistic romanticism to passionate sensuality, and in this collection we have gathered what we feel are the best examples of both extremes and every variation in between. The poems are arranged in a roughly thematic sequence, including poems of love at first sight, passionate attachment, mutual affection, marriage, and, sadly but inevitably, loss and remembrance. They include representatives from virtually every major language group and date from the early classic period of Greece and Rome up to the present day. Most poems included are complete, but a few are extracts from larger works. Some are examples of high art; others exemplify popular culture.

To maximize the breadth of the collection, while maintaining a convenient format suitable for browsing through or dipping into at an appropriate moment, we decided to include no more than one poem per poet, with the exception of William Shakespeare, whose Sonnet 18 ("Shall I Compare Thee to a Summer's Day?") is included primarily as a reference for Howard Moss's delightful modern gloss of the same title. As the juxtaposition of these two poems suggests, neither the historical period in which a poem is written nor the poetic tradition nor even the language it is written in affect the immediacy with which a great love poem instantly communicates emotion to the contemporary reader. Human nature after all does not change, and first love is as exhilarating and painful today as it was when Sappho wrote almost three thousand years ago "If I meet you suddenly, I can't speak"; passion today is as overwhelming as when Baudelaire wrote a century and a half ago of love that "was deep and gentle as the seas/And rose to her as to a cliff the tide."

The best love poems are those to which we respond by thinking, "That's the way it was for me!" Not every poem here will strike every reader in that way, since so many of love's diverse manifestations are represented. But each of these poems carries within it that same truth, expressed in different ways, for the reader who is, was, or hopes to be in love (which is all of us). And so it is our hope that this collection will speak to every reader, and reassure them that what they feel or felt is as universal as life itself.

This book would not have been possible without the early and enthusiastic support of Maureen Egen, Jamie Raab, and Amy Einhorn. Karen Melnyk and Sarah Rustin provided essential editorial contributions.

THE 100 BEST LOVE POEMS of ALL TIME

La Vita Nuova

DANTE ALIGHIERI

This is a brief excerpt from a larger work blending prose and poetry, in which Dante celebrates his idealized love for Beatrice. Even after seven hundred years it is easy to understand how a new life can seem to begin when lovers meet for the first time.

> In that book which is
> My memory . . .
> On the first page
> That is the chapter when
> I first met you
> Appear the words . . .
> Here begins a new life.

Shakespeare is the only poet to receive double recognition in this collection, in this case to supply a reference to Howard Moss's delightful contemporary version of his classic sonnet. Moss, for many years poetry editor of the New Yorker magazine, casts off traditional meter and rhyme in exchange for a colloquial style that expresses a heartfelt exuberance.

Shall I Compare Thee to a Summer's Day?

WILLIAM SHAKESPEARE

Shall I compare thee to a Summer's day?
Thou are more lovely and more temperate:
Rough winds do shake the darling buds of
    May,
And Summer's lease hath all too short a
    date:
Sometime too hot the eye of heaven
    shines,
And often is his gold complexion dimm'd;
And every fair from fair sometime declines,
By chance or nature's changing course
    untrimm'd:

But thy eternal Summer shall not fade
Nor lose possession of that fair thou ow'st;
Nor shall Death brag thou wander'st in his
    shade,
When in eternal lines to time thou grow'st:
So long as men can breathe, or eyes can
    see,
So long lives this, and this gives life to
    thee.

Shall I Compare Thee to a Summer's Day?

HOWARD MOSS

Who says you're like one of the dog days?
You're nicer. And better.
Even in May, the weather can be gray,
And a summer sub-let doesn't last forever.
Sometimes the sun's too hot;
Sometimes it is not.
Who can stay young forever?
People break their necks or just drop dead!
But you? Never!
If there's just one condensed reader left
Who can figure out the abridged alphabet,
 After you're dead and gone,
 In this poem you'll live on!

Who Ever Loved

CHRISTOPHER MARLOWE

Marlowe, Shakespeare's only real contemporary rival, is mostly remembered for his powerful verse dramas, such as Dr. Faustus. *This perceptive verse shows that he was also an eloquent poet and a keen psychologist of desire.*

It lies not in our power to love or hate,
For will in us is overruled by fate.
When two are stripped, long ere the course
    begin,
We wish that one should lose, the other
    win;
And one especially do we affect
Of two gold ingots, like in each respect:
The reason no man knows; let it suffice
What we behold is censored by our eyes.
Where both deliberate, the love is slight:
Who ever loved, that loved not at first
    sight?

From
Paradise Lost
(Book IV)

JOHN MILTON

In this tender monologue Eve tells Adam how none of the beauties and wonders of nature mean anything to her without him. Milton's gorgeous evocation of the pleasures of love in paradise makes the coming temptation and fall of the first man and woman seem all the more poignant.

With thee conversing I forget all time,
All seasons and their change, all please
   alike.
Sweet is the breath of morn, her rising
   sweet,
With charm of earliest birds; pleasant the
   sun
When first on this delightful land he
   spreads
His orient beams, on herb, tree, fruit, and
   flower,
Glistring with dew; fragrant the fertile earth
After soft showers; and sweet the coming
   on

Of grateful evening mild, then silent night
With this her solemn bird and this fair
    moon,
And these the gems of heav'n, her starry
    train:
But neither breath of morn when she
    ascends
With charm of earliest birds, nor rising sun
On this delightful land, nor herb, fruit,
    flower,
Glistring with dew, nor fragrance after
    showers,
Nor grateful evening mild, nor silent night
With this her solemn bird, nor walk by
    moon,
Or glittering starlight without thee is sweet.

To Helen

EDGAR ALLAN POE

Poe softens his customary pounding rhythms and repetitive rhymes in this delicately romantic evocation of classicism. The poem is an almost prayer-like adoration of a beloved figure, viewed from afar.

Helen, thy beauty is to me
　　Like those Nicéan barks of yore,
That gently, o'er a perfumed sea,
　　The weary, way-worn wanderer bore
　　To his own native shore.

On desperate seas long wont to roam,
　　Thy hyacinth hair, thy classic face,
Thy Naiad airs have brought me home
　　To the glory that was Greece,
　　And the grandeur that was Rome.

Lo! in yon brilliant window-niche
　　How statue-like I see thee stand,
The agate lamp within thy hand!
　　Ah, Psyche, from the regions which
　　Are Holy-Land!

A Red, Red Rose

ROBERT BURNS

This lyric by Scotland's greatest poet breathes life into a series of similes that sound as natural as a song, and as sincere as a prayer.

O my luve's like a red, red rose,
    That's newly sprung in June;
O my luve's like the melodie
    That's sweetly played in tune.

As fair art thou, my bonnie lass,
    So deep in luve am I;
And I will luve thee still, my dear,
    Till a' the seas gang dry.

Till a' the seas gang dry, my dear,
    And the rocks melt wi' the sun:
O I will love thee still, my dear,
    While the sands o' life shall run.

And fare thee weel, my only luve,
    And fare thee weel awhile!
And I will come again, my luve,
    Though it were ten thousand mile.

She Tells Her Love while Half Asleep

ROBERT GRAVES

A lover compares his drowsy loved one and her murmured endearments to early spring blossoms that emerge while the snow is still falling. The rhyme scheme and repetition at the end produce an almost hypnotic effect.

She tells her love while half asleep
In the dark hours,
With half-words whispered low;

As Earth stirs in her winter sleep
And puts out grass and flowers
Despite the snow,
Despite the falling snow.

Last Night You Left Me and Slept

RUMI

This greatest of all Sufi mystics and poets lived in thirteenth-century Afghanistan, but his love poems have a completely contemporary immediacy, as in this representation of two sharply contrasting sides of a relationship.

Last night you left me and slept
your own deep sleep. Tonight you turn
and turn. I say,
"You and I will be together
till the universe dissolves."
You mumble back things you thought of
when you were drunk.

I Prithee Send Me Back My Heart

SIR JOHN SUCKLING

Suckling was one of a group of so-called English cavalier poets in the Court of King Charles I. Here he playfully debates the merits of a heart-to-heart bargain between lovers.

I prithee send me back my heart,
Since I cannot have thine;
For if from yours you will not part,
Why then shouldst thou have mine?

Yet now I think on't, let it lie,—
To find it were in vain;
For thou'st a thief in either eye
Would steal it back again.

Why should two hearts in one breast lie,
And yet not lodge together?
O love, where is thy sympathy,
If thus our breasts thou sever?

But love is such a mystery,
I cannot find it out;
For when I think I'm best resolved,
I then am most in doubt.

Then farewell care, and farewell woe,—
I will no longer pine;
For I'll believe I have her heart
As much as she hath mine.

I Carry Your Heart with Me

E. E. CUMMINGS

Cummings is known for typographic and orthographic experimentation in his verse, but this should not obscure the genuine feeling—and, in this case, tenderness—that characterizes his best poetry.

i carry your heart with me(i carry it in
my heart)i am never without it(anywhere
i go you go, my dear;and whatever is done
by only me is your doing,my darling)
                        i fear
no fate(for you are my fate,my sweet)i
    want
no world(for beautiful you are my world,my
    true)
and it's you are whatever a moon has
    always meant
and whatever a sun will always sing is you

here is the deepest secret nobody knows
(here is the root of the root and the bud of
    the bud
and the sky of the sky of a tree called
    life;which grows

14

higher than soul can hope or mind can
    hide)
and this is the wonder that's keeping the
    stars apart

i carry your heart(i carry it in my heart)

The Avenue

FRANCES CORNFORD

Frances Cornford, a granddaughter of Charles Darwin, wrote often of the everyday life in and around Cambridge, England. Here she takes an ordinary street scene and turns it into a romantic epiphany.

Who has not seen their lover
Walking at ease,
Walking like any other
A pavement under trees,
Not singular, apart,
But footed, featured, dressed,
Approaching like the rest
In the same dapple of the summer caught;
Who has not suddenly thought
With swift surprise:
There walks in cool disguise,
There comes, my heart.

The Bargain

SIR PHILIP SIDNEY

Sir Philip Sidney was perhaps the ideal Renaissance man of England's Elizabethan Age. A soldier, statesman, and scholar, he was also a gifted lyric poet. "The Bargain" is a playful examination of a more-than-fair exchange in which both parties—and lovers—profit.

My true love hath my heart, and I have his,
    By just exchange one for another given:
I hold his dear, and mine he cannot miss,
      There never was a better bargain driven:
        My true love hath my heart, and I have
        his.

His heart in me keeps him and me in one,
    My heart in him his thoughts and senses
    guides:
He loves my heart, for once it was his own,
    I cherish his because in me it bides:
      My true love hath my heart, and I have
      his.

The Mirabeau Bridge

GUILLAUME APOLLINAIRE

The great French symbolist poet watches with his lover as the River Seine flows beneath them, representing love, longing, passion, and time itself. Yet time has no power while the lovers are bound within each other's shadow. The translation is by Quentin Stevenson.

Under the Mirabeau bridge the Seine
Flows with our loves;
Must I remember once again
Joy followed always after pain?
Night may come and clock may sound,
Within your shadow I am bound.

Clasp hand in hand, keep face to face,
Whilst here below
The bridge formed by our arms' embrace
The waters of our endless longing pass.
Night may come and clock may sound,
Within your shadow I am bound.

And like this stream our passions flow,
Our love goes by;

The violence hope dare not show
Follows time's beat which now falls slow.
Night may come and clock may sound,
Within your shadow I am bound.

The days move on; but still we strain
Back towards time past;
Still to waters of the Seine
We bend to catch the echo gone.
Night may come and clock may sound,
Within your shadow I am bound.

To the Bridge of Love

JUAN RAMON JIMENEZ

*As in Apollinaire's "The Mirabeau Bridge,"
this poem finds a metaphor for love in the
water passing beneath, passing but never
changing. The translation is by James
Wright.*

To the bridge of love,
old stone between tall cliffs
   —eternal meeting place, red evening—,
I come with my heart,
   —My beloved is only water,
that always passes away, and does not
     deceive,
that always passes away, and does not
     change,
that always passes away, and does not
     end.

She Walks in Beauty

LORD BYRON

Byron was said to have written this poem as an elaborate compliment the morning after meeting a beautiful woman.

She walks in beauty, like the night
    Of cloudless climes and starry skies;
And all that's best of dark and bright
    Meet in her aspect and her eyes:
Thus mellow'd to that tender light
    Which heaven to gaudy day denies.

One shade the more, one ray the less,
    Had half impair'd the nameless grace
Which waves in every raven tress,
    Or softly lightens o'er her face;
Where thoughts serenely sweet express
    How pure, how dear their dwelling-place.

And on that cheek, and o'er that brow,
    So soft, so calm, yet eloquent,
The smiles that win, the tints that glow,
    But tell of days in goodness spent,
A mind at peace with all below,
    A heart whose love is innocent!

The Ragged Wood

WILLIAM BUTLER YEATS

*This ballad-like lyric sings forth the unshake-
able belief of all lovers since the beginning
of time: "No one has ever loved but you
and I."*

O, hurry, where by water, among the trees,
The delicate-stepping stag and his lady
   sigh,
When they have looked upon their images
Would none had ever loved but you and I!

Or have you heard that sliding silver-shoed
Pale silver-proud queen-woman of the sky,
When the sun looked out of his golden
   hood?
O, that none ever loved but you and I!

O hurry to the ragged wood, for there
I will drive all those lovers out and cry
O, my share of the world, O, yellow hair!
No one has ever loved but you and I.

Night Thoughts

JOHANN WOLFGANG VON GOETHE

In "Night Thoughts" Goethe, a natural scientist as well as a poet, celebrates love's transcendence of the material universe. Indeed, gazing at the most beautiful stars in the heavens pales in comparison to "lingering in the arms" of the one you adore and love.

Stars, you are unfortunate, I pity you,
Beautiful as you are, shining in your glory,
Who guide seafaring men through stress
    and peril
And have no recompense from gods or
    mortals,
Love you do not, nor do you know what
    love is.
Hours that are aeons urgently conducting
Your figures in a dance through the vast
    heaven,
What journey have you ended in this
    moment,
Since lingering in the arms of my beloved
I lost all memory of you and midnight.

The Gardener

RABINDRANATH TAGORE

Tagore himself translated this poem into English from its original Bengali version. Its highly metaphorical and almost reverent exploration of the essence of love is both redolent of its origins and universal in its impact.

Your questioning eyes are sad.
They seek to know my meaning
as the moon would fathom the sea.
I have bared my life before your eyes from
   end to end,
with nothing hidden or held back.
That is why you know me not.
If it were only a gem,
I could break it into a hundred pieces
and string them into a chain to put on your
   neck.
If it were only a flower, round and small
   and sweet,
I could pluck it from its stem to set it in
   your hair.
But it is a heart, my beloved.
Where are its shores and its bottom?

You know not the limits of this kingdom,
still you are its queen.
If it were only a moment of pleasure
it would flower in an easy smile,
and you could see it and read it in a
    moment.
If it were merely a pain it would melt in
    limpid tears,
reflecting its inmost secret without a word.
But it is love, my beloved.
Its pleasure and pain are boundless,
and endless its wants and wealth.
It is as near to you as your life,
but you can never wholly know it.

To the Harbormaster

FRANK O'HARA

*Love is not mentioned in this allusive poem,
but the ship driven through "terrible channels" is clearly sailing with great difficulty
toward a safe harbor it wants very much to
reach. The calmness of the poem's conver-
sational voice, so typical of O'Hara's work, is
belied by the evident desperation of the
ship's struggle toward home.*

I wanted to be sure to reach you;
though my ship was on the way it got
   caught
in some moorings. I am always tying up
and then deciding to depart. In storms and
at sunset, with the metallic coils of the tide
around my fathomless arms, I am unable
to understand the forms of my vanity
or I am hard alee with my Polish rudder
in my hand and the sun sinking. To
you I offer my hull and the tattered cordage
of my will. The terrible channels where
the wind drives me against the brown lips
of the reeds are not all behind me. Yet
I trust the sanity of my vessel; and

if it sinks it may well be in answer
to the reasoning of the eternal voices,
the waves which have kept me from
    reaching you.

To a Stranger

WALT WHITMAN

In "To a Stranger," Whitman expresses a general sense of longing directed at the world in general. Nostalgic for past relationships and conscious of having his feelings of affection reciprocated by everyone he walks past, he knows he'll ultimately find love.

Passing stranger! you do not know
How longingly I look upon you,
You must be he I was seeking,
Or she I was seeking
(It comes to me as a dream)

I have somewhere surely
Lived a life of joy with you,
All is recall'd as we flit by each other,
Fluid, affectionate, chaste, matured,

You grew up with me,
Were a boy with me or a girl with me,
I ate with you and slept with you, your
   body has become
not yours only nor left my body mine only,

You give me the pleasure of your eyes,
face, flesh as we pass,
You take of my beard, breast, hands,
in return,

I am not to speak to you, I am to think of you
when I sit alone or wake at night, alone
I am to wait, I do not doubt I am to meet
    you again
I am to see to it that I do not lose you.

True Love

JUDITH VIORST

This lilting, colloquial verse takes the style of Walt Whitman and infuses it with the spirit of a married woman of a certain age, celebrating the song of herself, her husband, and their still vital relationship.

It is true love because
I put on eyeliner and a concerto and make
    pungent observations about the great
    issues of the day
Even when there's no one here but him,
And because
I do not resent watching the Green Bay
    Packers
Even though I am philosophically opposed to
    football,
And because
When he is late for dinner and I know he must
    be either having an affair or lying dead in
    the middle of the street,
I always hope he's dead.
It's true love because
If he said quit drinking martinis but I kept
    drinking them and the next morning I
    couldn't get out of bed,

He wouldn't tell me he told me,
And because
He is willing to wear unironed undershorts
Out of respect for the fact that I am
    philosophically opposed to ironing,
And because
If his mother was drowning and I was
    drowning and he had to choose one of us
    to save,
He says he'd save me.
It's true love because
When he went to San Francisco on business
    while I had to stay home with the painters
    and the exterminator and the baby who
    was getting the chicken pox,
He understood why I hated him,
And because
When I said that playing the stock market was
    juvenile and irresponsible and then the
    stock I wouldn't let him buy went up
    twenty-six points,
I understood why he hated me,
And because
Despite cigarette cough, tooth decay, acid
    indigestion, dandruff, and other features of

married life that tend to dampen the fires of
passion,
We still feel something
We can call
True love.

Love 20 Cents the First Quarter Mile

KENNETH FEARING

It's been a long time since the initial charge for a New York taxi was twenty cents, but the hardboiled yet tender, bantering tone of this plea for reconciliation is completely imbued with the spirit of the City that Never Sleeps.

All right. I may have lied to you and about
you, and made a few pronouncements a
bit too sweeping,
perhaps, and possibly forgotten to tag the
bases here or there,
And damned your extravagance, and
maligned your tastes, and libeled your
relatives, and slandered a few of your
friends,
O.K.,
Nevertheless, come back.

Come home. I will agree to forget the
statements that you issued so copiously
to the neighbors and the press,
And you will forget that figment of your
imagination, the blonde from Detroit;

I will agree that your lady friend who lives
above us is not crazy, bats, nutty as they
come,
but on the contrary rather bright,
And you will concede that poor Steinberg
is neither a drunk, nor a swindler, but
simply a guy, on the
eccentric side, trying to get along.
(Are you listening, you b . . . , and have you
got this straight?)

Because I forgive you, yes, for everything.
I forgive you for being beautiful and
generous and wise,
I forgive you, to put it simply, for being
alive, and pardon you, in short, for being
you.

Because tonight you are in my hair and
eyes,
And every street light that our taxi passes
shows me you again, still you,
And because tonight all other nights are
black, all other hours are cold and far
away,

34

and now,
this minute, the stars are very near and
bright.

Come back. We will have a celebration to
end all celebrations.
We will invite the undertaker who lives
beneath us, and a couple of boys from
the office, and some other friends.
And Steinberg, who is off the wagon, and
that insane woman who lives upstairs,
and a
few reporters,
if anything should break.

Jenny Kiss'd Me

LEIGH HUNT

Leigh Hunt was a nineteenth-century British poet and critic who counted many notable figures among his friends. The Jenny of this poem was the wife of the historian and essayist Thomas Carlyle.

Jenny kiss'd me when we met,
    Jumping from the chair she sat in;
Time, you thief, who love to get
    Sweets into your list, put that in!
Say I'm weary, say I'm sad,
    Say that health and wealth have miss'd
     me,
Say I'm growing old, but add,
    Jenny kiss'd me.

Juliet

HILAIRE BELLOC

Belloc was famous for his epigrammatic wit. Here he concisely conveys a sense of complete, head-over-heels infatuation.

How did the party go in Portman Square?
I cannot tell you: Juliet was not there.

And how did Lady Gaster's party go?
Juliet was next to me and I do not know.

Song to Celia

BEN JONSON

Jonson was Shakespeare's contemporary and in his lifetime was ranked nearly as high as a poet and playwright. This familiar poem also provides the words to a well-known love song.

Drink to me, only, with thine eyes,
    And I will pledge with mine;
Or leave a kiss but in the cup,
    And I'll not look for wine.
The thirst that from the soul doth rise,
    Doth ask a drink divine:
But might I of Jove's nectar sup,
    I would not change for thine.

I sent thee, late, a rosy wreath,
    Not so much honoring thee,
As giving it a hope, that there
    It could not wither'd be.
But thou thereon didst only breathe,
    And sent'st it back to me:
Since when it grows, and smells, I swear,
    Not of itself, but thee.

Your Catfish Friend

RICHARD BRAUTIGAN

It's been said, "Brautigan is good for you."
His wit and sensitivity encourage the catfish
in all of us who love or have loved from afar
to gain confidence and take a chance on the
one who stands at the edge of our affection.

If I were to live my life
in catfish forms
in scaffolds of skin and whiskers
at the bottom of a pond
and you were to come by
   one evening
when the moon was shining
down into my dark home
and stand there at the edge
   of my affection
and think, "It's beautiful
here by this pond. I wish
   somebody loved me,"
I'd love you and be your catfish
friend and drive such lonely
thoughts from your mind
and suddenly you would be
   at peace,

and ask yourself, "I wonder
if there are any catfish
in this pond? It seems like
a perfect place for them."

The Owl and the Pussy-Cat

EDWARD LEAR

"The Owl and the Pussy-Cat" exemplifies nonsense poetry. Lear, in delightfully musical versification, shows us a topsy-turvy world where even the most unlikely of couples is lucky in love.

The Owl and the Pussy-cat went to sea
  In a beautiful pea-green boat,
They took some honey, and plenty of
      money,
  Wrapped up in a five-pound note.
The Owl looked up to the stars above,
  And sang to a small guitar,
"O lovely Pussy! O Pussy, my love,
  What a beautiful Pussy you are,
    You are,
    You are!
What a beautiful Pussy you are!"

Pussy said to the Owl, "You elegant fowl!
  How charmingly sweet you sing!
O let us be married! too long we have
      tarried:
  But what shall we do for a ring?"

They sailed away, for a year and a day,
    To the land where the Bong-Tree grows,
And there in a wood a Piggy-wig stood,
    With a ring at the end of his nose,
        His nose,
        His nose,
With a ring at the end of his nose.

"Dear Pig, are you willing to sell for one
        shilling
    Your ring?" Said the Piggy, "I will."
So they took it away, and were married
        next day
    By the Turkey who lives on the hill.
They dined on mince, and slices of quince,
    Which they ate with a runcible spoon;
And hand in hand, on the edge of the
        sand,
    They danced by the light of the moon,
        The moon,
        The moon,
They danced by the light of the moon.

Love Song to Alex, 1979

MARGARET WALKER

Various elements of a relationship can keep it strong and intact. In this poem Walker proposes devotion as the key piece in the intricate puzzle that holds her and her monkey-wrench man together.

My monkey-wrench man is my sweet
 patootie;
the lover of my life, my youth and age.
My heart belongs to him and to him
 only;
the children of my flesh are his and bear
 his rage.
Now grown to years advancing through the
 dozens
the honeyed kiss, the lips of wine and
 fire
fade blissfully into the distant years of
 yonder
but all my days of Happiness and wonder
are cradled in his arms and eyes entire.
They carry us under the waters of the
 world
out past the starposts of a distant planet

And creeping through the seaweed of the
    ocean
they tangle us with ropes and yarn of
    memories
where we have been together, you and I.

When Sue Wears Red

LANGSTON HUGHES

The poet here uses the form and some of the language of a testifying preacher to sing the praises of an earthly—if classic—beauty.

When Susanna Jones wears red
Her face is like an ancient cameo
Turned brown by the age.

Come with a blast of trumpets,
Jesus!

When Susanna Jones wears red
A queen from some time-dead Egyptian
    night
Walks once again.

Blow trumpets, Jesus!

And the beauty of Susanna Jones in red
Burns in my heart a love-fire sharp like
    pain.

Sweet silver trumpets,
Jesus!

Those Who Love

SARA TEASDALE

Not enough can be said about true love to do it justice, and so as a rule it is better kept private and unspoken. Still, what the heart feels is difficult to contain, and although words don't speak loudly enough, actions can and always do.

Those who love the most,
Do not talk of their love,
Francesca, Guinevere,
Deirdre, Iseult, Heloise,
In the fragrant gardens of heaven
Are silent, or speak if at all
Of fragile inconsequent things.

And a woman I used to know
Who loved one man from her youth,
Against the strength of the fates
Fighting in somber pride
Never spoke of this thing,
But hearing his name by chance,
A light would pass over her face.

Reprise

OGDEN NASH

Nash was famous for the wordplay and convoluted rhyme schemes of his humorous poetry, but here he gets serious for a moment, to touching effect. Perhaps everything about love and lovers has already been said, but every time two people fall in love, the familiar phrases all gain renewed meaning.

Geniuses of countless nations
Have told their love for generations
Till all their memorable phrases
Are common as goldenrod or daisies.
Their girls have glimmered like the moon,
Or shimmered like a summer moon,
Stood like a lily, fled like a fawn,
Now the sunset, now the dawn,
Here the princess in the tower
There the sweet forbidden flower.
Darling, when I look at you
Every aged phrase is new,
And there are moments when it seems
I've married one of Shakespeare's dreams.

One Word Is Too Often Profaned

PERCY BYSSHE SHELLEY

Shelley was never one to follow convention, and this love poem explicitly repudiates love for something the poet feels is even more profound: an adoration that transcends the world's imperfection and aspires to a higher state of being.

One word is too often profaned
    For me to profane it,
One feeling too falsely disdained
    For thee to disdain it;
One hope is too like despair
    For prudence to smother,
And pity from thee more dear
    Than that from another.

I can give not what men call love,
    But wilt thou accept not
The worship the heart lifts above
    And the Heavens reject not,—
The desire of the moth for the star,
    Of the night for the morrow,
The devotion to something afar
    From the sphere of our sorrow?

I Do Not Love You

PABLO NERUDA

Neruda's third wife, Matilde Urrutia, was the inspiration for many of the verses he wrote in 100 Love Sonnets. *There is a strong sense that the love he speaks of in this poem is what he experienced with Matilde. Something passionate and profound, but also easy and natural . . .*

I do not love you as if you were salt-rose,
    or topaz,
or the arrow of carnations the fire shoots
    off.
I love you as certain dark things are to be
    loved,
in secret, between the shadow and the
    soul.

I love you as the plant that never blooms
but carries in itself the light of hidden
    flowers;
thanks to your love a certain solid
    fragrance,
risen from the earth, lives darkly in my
    body.

I love you without knowing how, or when,
   or from where.
I love you straightforwardly, without
   complexities or pride;
so I love you because I know no other way

than this: where *I* does not exist, nor *you,*
so close that your hand on my chest is my
   hand,
so close that your eyes close as I fall
   asleep.

Gifts

JULIANA HORATIA EWING

In June 1867 Juliana married army captain Alexander Ewing. Although they began their life and travels together, she eventually became ill and around 1879 returned to London, while her husband continued to be transferred around the world. "Gifts" illuminates Juliana's thoughts during those years apart.

You ask me what since we must part
You shall bring back to me.
Bring back a pure and faithful heart
As true as mine to thee.

You talk of gems from foreign lands,
Of treasure, spoil, and prize.
Ah love! I shall not search your hands
But look into your eyes.

At Last

ELIZABETH AKERS ALLEN

Timing is everything, especially in matters of the heart. "At Last" tells of a deferred love affair—when the two lovers finally unite in their later years, their love is ultimately stronger than it ever could have been before, because the depths of their affection have been tested by time.

At last, when all the summer shine
    That warmed life's early hours is past,
Your loving fingers seek for mine
    And hold them close—at last—at last!
Not oft the robin comes to build
    Its nest upon the leafless bough
By autumn robbed, by winter chilled,—
    But you, dear heart, you love me now.

Though there are shadows on my brow
    And furrows on my cheek, in truth,—
The marks where Time's remorseless
      plough
    Broke up the blooming sward of
      Youth,—
Though fled is every girlish grace

Might win or hold a lover's vow,
Despite my sad and faded face,
  And darkened heart, you love me now!

I count no more my wasted tears;
  They left no echo of their fall;
I mourn no more my lonesome years;
  This blessed hour atones for all.
I fear not all that Time or Fate
  May bring to burden heart or brow,—
Strong in the love that came so late,
Our souls shall keep it always now!

To Alice B. Toklas

GERTRUDE STEIN

Stein is famous for her support of cubism in its early years and her attempts to apply this artistic theory to writing. As a result, the meaning of much of her work is difficult to penetrate, but this passionate affirmation of love is as clear as crystal.

Do you really think I would yes I would and
I do love all you with all me.
Do you really think I could, yes I could
yes I would love all you with all me.
Do you really think I should yes I should
love all you with all me yes I should
yes I could yes I would.
Do you really think I do love all you
with all me yes I do love all you with all
me And bless my baby.

Valentine

DONALD HALL

This Valentine sentiment is playful but heart-felt. The poem's vitality and power are heightened by the alternation of colorful images of animals in motion with the poet's fervent declarations of love.

Chipmunks jump, and
Greensnakes slither.
Rather burst than
Not be with her.

Bluebirds fight, but
Bears are stronger.
We've got fifty
Years or longer.

Hoptoads hop, but
Hogs are fatter.
Nothing else but
Us can matter.

Love's Secret

WILLIAM BLAKE

Blake was a mystical poet with more faith in sincere feelings than intellectual discourse. Perhaps the message here is that words can do more harm than good, and that true love is best expressed in other ways.

Never seek to tell thy love,
Love that never told can be;
For the gentle wind doth move
Silently, invisibly.

I told my love, I told my love,
I told her all my heart,
Trembling, cold, in ghastly fears,
Ah! She did depart!

Soon after she was gone from me,
A traveler came by,
Silently, invisibly:
He took her with a sigh.

I Knew a Woman

THEODORE ROETHKE

This poem is a lyrical celebration of a man's love of, and submission to, a woman's physical charms. The repetitive rhyme scheme of the last lines of each stanza give the entire work a playful, almost childlike tone, though the subject is anything but.

I knew a woman, lovely in her bones,
When small birds sighed, she would sigh
  back at them;
Ah, when she moved, she moved more
  ways than one:
The shapes a bright container can
  contain!
Of her choice virtues only gods could
  speak,
Or English poets who grew up on Greek
(I'd have them sing in chorus, cheek to
  cheek).

How well her wishes went! She stroked my
  chin,
She taught me Turn, and Counter-turn, and
  Stand,

She taught me Touch, that undulant white
  skin;
I nibbled meekly from her proffered hand;
She was the sickle; I, poor I, the rake,
Coming behind her for her pretty sake
(But what prodigious mowing we did
  make).

Love likes a gander, and adores a goose:
Her full lips pursued, the errant note to
  seize;
She played it quick, she played it light and
  loose;
My eyes, they dazzled at her flowing
  knees;
Her several parts could keep a pure
  repose,
Or one hip quiver with a mobile nose
(She moved in circles, and those circles
  moved).

Let seed be grass, and grass turn into hay;
I'm martyr to a motion not my own;
What's freedom for? To know eternity.
I swear she cast a shadow white as stone.

But who would count eternity in days?
These old bones live to learn her wanton
    ways:
(I measure time by how a body sways).

Love for a Hand

KARL SHAPIRO

This poem about a dream is itself dreamlike in its sudden yet quiet shifts in time, place, and reality. The hands of the husband and wife become almost living expressions of their love, and their union an ultimate consummation.

Two hands lie still, the hairy and the white,
And soon down ladders of reflected lights
The sleepers climb in silence. Gradually
They separate on paths of long ago,
Each winding on his arm the unpleasant
    clew
That leads, live as a nerve, to memory.

But often when too steep her dream
    descends,
Perhaps to the grotto where her father
    bends
To pick her up, the husband wakes as
    though
He had forgotten something in the house.
Motionless he eyes the room that glows
With the little animals of light that prowl

This way and that, soft are the beasts of
    light
But softer still her hand that drifts so white
Upon the whiteness. How like a water-
    plant
It floats upon the black canal of sleep,
Suspended upward from the distant deep
In pure achievement of its lovely want!

Quietly then he plucks it and it folds
And is again a hand, small as a child's.
He would revive it but it barely stirs
And so he carries it off a little way
And breaks it open gently. Now he can see
The sweetness of the fruit, and his hand
    eats hers.

It Is the Third Watch

ANONYMOUS

Written in the sixteenth century by an unknown Korean poet, this poem offers a husband's ecstatic vision of his wedding night and his lovely teenaged bride. There is passion here, clearly, but also the promise that this is just the beginning of the happy marriage of a well-matched pair.

It is the third watch. The girl
    in the bridal bedroom is so gentle,
    so beautiful, I look and look again;
    I can't believe my eyes.
Sixteen years old, peach blossom
  complexion,
    golden hairpin, white ramie skirt,
    bright eyes agleam in playful glance,
    lips half-parted in a smile.
    My love! My own true love!
Need I say ought
    of the silver in her voice
    and the wonder of her under the quilt.

The Enchantment

THOMAS OTWAY

In this charming lyric, the poet complains that he has lost all willpower and sighs all day for want of a little attention from his lover. And yet, while the poet is complaining all the while, the bouncy verse seems to show he's as cheerful a helpless lover as could be imagined.

I did but look and love a while,
'Twas but for one half-hour;
Then to resist I had no will,
And now I have no power.

To sigh and wish is all my ease;
Sighs, which do heat, impart,
Enough to melt the coldest ice,
Yet cannot warm your heart.

Oh! Would your pity give my heart
One corner of your breast,
'Twould learn of yours the winning art,
And quickly steal the rest.

The Silken Tent

ROBERT FROST

Winner of four Pulitzer Prizes, Robert Frost was one of the most esteemed American poets of the twentieth century. In "Silken Tent," Frost combines a centuries-old poetic form—the sonnet—with the distinctly modern allegiance to colloquial language that is a defining characteristic of his work. Frost, a master of metaphor, creates a superbly sensuous effect in his description of a woman moving like a silken tent in a summer breeze.

She is as in a field a silken tent
At midday, when a sunny summer breeze
Has dried the dew, and all its ropes relent
So that in guys it gently sways at ease
And its supporting central cedar pole
That is its pinnacle to heavenward
And signifies the sureness of the soul
Seems to owe naught to any single cord
But, strictly held by none, is loosely
    bound
By countless silken ties of love and
    thought

To everything on earth the compass 'round
And only by one going slightly taut
In the capriciousness of summer air
Is of the slightest bondage made aware.

Love Song

WILLIAM CARLOS WILLIAMS

Williams was a poet of the senses, creating chains of images that together evoke profound feelings. Here colors, especially tones of yellow, purple, and dark red, combine to express longing for a distant beloved.

I lie here thinking of you:—

the stain of love
is upon the world!
Yellow, yellow, yellow
it eats into the leaves,
smears with saffron
the horned branches that lean
heavily
against a smooth purple sky!
There is no light
only a honey-thick stain
that drips from leaf to leaf
and limb to limb

spoiling the colors
of the whole world—

you far off there under
the wine-red selvage of the west!

Wild Nights!
EMILY DICKINSON

This deceptively simple verse captures the ambiguity of Emily Dickinson's passions. The dual passions that ruled the poet's life—the physical and the spiritual—are often difficult to distinguish in her writing.

Wild nights! Wild nights!
Were I with thee,
Wild nights should be
Our luxury!

Futile the winds
To a heart in port—
Done with the compass,
Done with the chart.

Rowing in Eden!
Ah! The sea!
Might I but moor
Tonight in thee!

She Comes Not When Noon Is on the Roses

HERBERT TRENCH

This love is not for everyday use. Trench depicts a love too delicate, too ethereal to occupy the material world. The object of his love appears as a dream and thus remains exquisitely pure.

She comes not when Noon is on the
    roses—
. . . Too bright is Day.
She comes not to the Soul till it reposes
. . . From work and play.

But when Night is on the hills, and the
    great Voices
. . . Roll in from Sea,
By starlight and by candlelight and
    dreamlight
. . . She comes to me.

Between Your Sheets

LADY MARY WORTLEY MONTAGU

Lady Mary was a woman ahead of her time (the eighteenth century), especially in her advanced views on a woman's proper role in society. This poem exhibits a sexual frankness and sensuality that seems quite contemporary, despite its period style.

Between your sheets you soundly sleep
Nor dream of vigils that we lovers keep
While all the night, I waking sigh your
    name,
The tender sound does every nerve
    inflame.
Imagination shows me all your charms,
The plenteous silken hair, and waxen arms,
And all the beauties that supinely rest
. . . between your sheets.

Ah Lindamira, could you see my heart,
How fond, how true, how free from fraudful
    art,
The warmest glances poorly do explain
The eager wish, the melting throbbing
    pain

Which through my very blood and soul I
    feel,
Which you cannot believe nor I reveal,
Which every metaphor must render less
And yet (methinks) which I could well
    express
. . . between your sheets.

The Jewels

CHARLES BAUDELAIRE

*The explicit sensual power of this poem is
such that a reader might feel the need of a
cold shower after reading it. The translation
is by Roy Campbell.*

My well-beloved was stripped. Knowing
   my whim,
She wore her tinkling gems, but naught
   besides:
And showed such pride as, while her luck
   betides,
A sultan's favored slave may show to him.

When it lets off its lively, crackling sound,
This blazing blend of metal crossed with
   stone,
Gives me an ecstasy I've only known
Where league of sound and luster can be
   found.

She let herself be loved: then, drowsy-
   eyed,
Smiled down from her high couch in
   languid ease.

My love was deep and gentle as the seas
And rose to her as to a cliff the tide.

My own approval of each dreamy pose,
Like a tamed tiger, cunningly she sighted:
And candour, with lubricity united,
Gave piquancy to every one she chose.

Her limbs and hips, burnished with
    changing lusters,
Before my eyes clairvoyant and serene,
Swanned themselves, undulating in their
    sheen;
Her breasts and belly, of my vine the
    clusters,

Like evil angels rose, my fancy twitting,
To kill the peace which over me she'd
    thrown,
And to disturb her from the crystal throne
Where, calm and solitary, she was sitting.

So swerved her pelvis that, in one
    design,
Antiope's white rump it seemed to graft

To a boy's torso, merging fore and aft.
The talc on her brown tan seemed half-
    divine.

The lamp resigned its dying flame. Within,
The hearth alone lit up the darkened air,
And every time it sighed a crimson flare
It drowned in blood that amber-colored
    skin.

Song 5 to Lesbia

CATULLUS (GAIUS VALERIUS CATULLUS)

In his brief life Catullus built a reputation for expressing passionate feelings with wit and lyricism that continues to this day. This translation is by the seventeenth-century English poet Richard Crashaw.

Come and let us live my Deare,
Let us love and never feare,
What the sourest Fathers say:
Brightest *Sol* that dyes to day
Lives againe as blith to morrow,
But if we darke sons of sorrow
Set; O then, how long a Night
Shuts the Eyes of our short light!
Then let amorous kisses dwell
On our lips, begin and tell
A Thousand, and a Hundred score
An Hundred, and a Thousand more,
Till another Thousand smother
That, and that wipe off another.
Thus at last when we have numbered
Many a Thousand, many a Hundred;
We'll confound the reckoning quite,
And lose our selves in wild delight:
While our joyes so multiply,
As shall mock the envious eye.

The Vine

JAMES THOMSON

Thomson led a rather unhappy life—he was depressive, alcoholic, and generally pessimistic about the world at large. And yet this poem is a ringing, joyful salute to the power of Love, drunk with its own vitality and passion.

The wine of Love is music,
. . . And the feast of Love is song:
And when Love sits down to the banquet,
. . . Love sits long:

Sits long and arises drunken,
. . . But not with the feast and the wine;
He reeleth with his own heart,
. . . That great, rich Vine.

From
The Song of Songs
ANONYMOUS
(ATTRIBUTED TO KING SOLOMON)

This excerpt from the classic love song, studded with memorable lines and images, is from the second chapter of the biblical work. Whether interpreted as an allegorical adoration of God or a frank expression of human love, the passionate lyricism of these verses is undeniable.

I am the rose of Sharon, and the lily of the valleys.

As the lily among thorns, so is my love among the daughters.

As the apple tree among the trees of the wood, so is my beloved among the sons. I sat down under his shadow with great delight, and his fruit was sweet to my taste.

He brought me to the banqueting house, and his banner over me was love.

Stay me with flagons, comfort me with apples: for I am sick of love.

His left hand is under my head, and his right hand doth embrace me.

I charge you, O ye daughters of Jerusalem, by the roes, and by the hinds of the field, that ye stir not up, nor awake my love, till he please.

The voice of my beloved! behold, he cometh leaping upon the mountains, skipping upon the hills.

My beloved is like a roe or a young hart: behold, he standeth behind our wall, he looketh forth at the windows, showing himself through the lattice.

My beloved spake, and said unto me, Rise up, my love, my fair one, and come away.

For, lo, the winter is past, the rain is over and gone;

The flowers appear on the earth; the time of the singing of birds is come, and the voice of the turtle is heard in our land:

The fig tree putteth forth her green figs, and the vines with the tender grape give a good smell. Arise, my love, my fair one, and come away.

Confession

FRANTISEK HALAS

Some people are ambivalent about love—it demands so much of us, and leaves us so vulnerable. This poem conveys some of the twists and turns on the path to trust.

Touched by all that love is
I draw closer toward you
Saddened by all that love is
I run from you

Surprised by all that love is
I remain alert in stillness
Hurt by all that love is
I yearn for tenderness

Defeated by all that love is
At the truthful mouth of the night
Forsaken by all that love is
I will grow toward you.

I Loved You

ALEXANDER SERGEYEVICH PUSHKIN

It's a cruel fact that love is never quite as easy to fall out of as it is to fall in—feelings linger long after we've said goodbye. Pushkin is known as Russia's greatest poet. At the age of thirty-eight he was tragically killed in a duel with a man reputed to be his wife's lover.

I loved you, and I probably still do,
And for a while the feeling may remain . . .
But let my love no longer trouble you,
I do not wish to cause you any pain.
I loved you; and the hopelessness I knew,
The jealousy, the shyness—though in
   vain—
Made up a love so tender and so true
As may God grant you to be loved again.

From
Merciless Beauty
GEOFFREY CHAUCER

Chaucer is generally regarded as the greatest English poet before Shakespeare. The rhythmic alternation and repetition of the beginning and ending lines emphasizes the narrator's sense of helplessness before his lover's beauty.

Your eyen two will slay me suddenly;
I may the beauty of them not sustain,
So woundeth it throughout my hearte keen.

And but your word will healen hastily
My hearte's wounde, while that it is green,
Your eyen two will slay me suddenly;
I may the beauty of them not sustain.

Upon my truth I say you faithfully
That ye bin of my life and death the queen;
For with my death the truthe shall be seen.
Your eyen two will slay me suddenly;
I may the beauty of them not sustain,
So woundeth it throughout my hearte keen.

He Is More than a Hero

SAPPHO

*Only fragments remain of the lyrical work of
this legendary poet, many of them poems of
friendship and love of other women. Despite
its title, this is one such poem.*

He is a god in my eyes—
the man who is allowed
to sit beside you—he

who listens intimately
to the sweet murmur of
your voice, the enticing

laughter that makes my own
heart beat fast. If I meet
you suddenly, I can't

speak—my tongue is broken;
a thin flame runs under
my skin; seeing nothing,

hearing only my own ears
drumming, I drip with sweat;
trembling shakes my body

and I turn paler than
dry grass. At such times
death isn't far from me.

To His Mistress

JOHN WILMOT, EARL OF ROCHESTER

Well known as a rakish wit in the Court of King Charles II, Rochester here deftly plays word games with comparisons of the sun's light and his love, the light of his life.

Why dost thou shade thy lovely face? O
   why
Does that eclipsing hand of thine deny
The sunshine of the Sun's enlivening eye?

Without thy light what light remains in me?
Thou art my life; my way, my light's in thee;
I live, I move, and by thy beams I see.

Thou art my life—if thou but turn away
My life's a thousand deaths. Thou art my
   way
Without thee, Love, I travel not but stray.

My light thou art—without thy glorious
   sight
My eyes are darken'd with eternal night.
My Love, thou art my way, my life, my
   light.

To Little or No Purpose

SIR GEORGE ETHEREGE

Etherege was famous in his own day (the seventeenth century) as a dramatist, for such romantic comedies as Love in a Tub *and* The Man of Mode, or Sir Fopling Flutter. *Today these plays are largely forgotten, but his charming, lyrical love poems are still prized. Here he writes in the voice of a lovesick young woman, not sure how long her fever will last, not willing to be free of it.*

To little or no purpose I spent many days
In ranging the park, the Exchange and the
    plays,
For ne'er in my rambles till now did I prove
So lucky to meet with the man I could
    love.

Oh, how I am pleased when I think on this
    man
That I find I must love, let me do what I
    can.
How long I shall love him I can no more
    tell
Than, had I a fever, when I should be well.

My passion shall kill me before I will show
    it,
And yet I would give all the world he did
    know it.
But oh! how I sigh when I think should he
    woo me
I cannot deny what I know would undo me.

Touch

OCTAVIO PAZ

In "Touch," Paz presents a world in which a moment of passion can transcend the two people involved. So absorbed in their senses is this couple that they achieve a state of intensity in which they are no longer themselves but something far greater.

My hands
Open the curtains of your being
Clothe you in a further nudity
Uncover the bodies of your body
My hands
Invent another body for your body

Lady Love

SAMUEL BECKETT

This poem, adapted from a work by the French surrealist poet Paul Eluard, is a rhapsodic song of praise to a lover whose presence virtually turns the narrator inside out with happiness.

She is standing on my lids
And her hair is in my hair
She has the colour of my eye
She has the body of my hand
In my shade she is engulfed
As a stone against the sky

She will never close her eyes
And she does not let me sleep
And her dreams in the bright day
Make the suns evaporate
And me laugh cry and laugh
Speak when I have nothing to say

Love Poem

GREGORY ORR

Inspired by the French Surrealists, Orr here creates a powerful scene that seems to have been taken from a dream. In this poem love causes physical and emotional disorder, which resolves itself in a harmonious simplicity. Love, like a dream, is not logical and has its reasons, which reason does not know.

A black biplane crashes through the
   window
of the luncheonette. The pilot climbs down,
removing his leather hood.
He hands me my grandmother's jade ring.
No, it is two robin's eggs and
a telephone number: yours.

I Want to Breathe

JAMES LAUGHLIN

Aside from his career as a notable poet, James Laughlin founded the publishing company New Directions, which over the years has published a distinguished list of authors, including William Carlos Williams, Lawrence Ferlinghetti, Ezra Pound, and many others. Laughlin's own poetry is characterized by an understated grace that has been considered distinctly American in the simplicity of its form.

I want to breathe

you in I'm not talking about
perfume or even the sweet odour

of your skin but of the
air itself I want to share

your air inhaling what you
exhale I'd like to be that

close two of us breathing
each other as one as that.

A Statue of Eros

ZENODOTOS

This poetic epigram (or epigrammatic poem) is an ironic commentary on the all-consuming power of passion. The translation is by Peter Jay.

Who carved Love
and placed him by
this fountain,
thinking
he could control
such fire
with water?

Come Quickly

IZUMI SHIKIBU

Love now, for life is fleeting, is the implicit message of this gemlike verse. The evanescence of existence is an essential component of Japanese esthetics, influenced by the tenets of Buddhism.

Come quickly—as soon as
these blossoms open,
they fall.
The world exists
As a sheen of dew on flowers

Let Me Not to the Marriage of True Minds

WILLIAM SHAKESPEARE

Shakespeare states that true love is unfaltering, sincere, and can overcome any obstacle. As much as a star is constant and guides wandering ships through rough waters, love does not vanish in the face of difficulty.

Let me not to the marriage of true minds
Admit impediments. Love is not love
Which alters when it alteration finds,
Or bends with the remover to remove:
O no! it is an ever-fixed mark
That looks on tempests and is never shaken;
It is the star to every wandering bark,
Whose worth's unknown, although his height
    be taken.
Love's not Time's fool, though rosy lips and
    cheeks
Within his bending sickle's compass come:
Love alters not with his brief hours and
    weeks,
But bears it out even to the edge of doom.
    If this be error and upon me proved,
    I never writ, nor no man ever loved.

Habitation

MARGARET ATWOOD

Rather than viewing marriage as a kind of shelter, Atwood depicts it as a journey through uncharted territory, by which a couple evolves past mere survival.

Marriage is not
a house or even a tent

it is before that, and colder:

the edge of the forest, the edge
of the desert
the unpainted stairs
at the back where we squat
outside, eating popcorn

the edge of the receding glacier

where painfully and with wonder
at having survived even
this far

we are learning to make fire

The following two poets were famously married. She committed suicide after he left her for another woman, who also killed herself. Their poems here both deal (in very different ways) with the transformational power of love. His takes its departure from the very end of summer, and hers from the very beginning of spring, yet both sharply communicate the pain as well as the ecstasy of two lovers' union.

September

TED HUGHES

We sit late, watching the dark slowly unfold:
No clock counts this.
When kisses are repeated and the arms
hold
There is no telling where time is.

It is midsummer: the leaves hang big and
still:
Behind the eye a star,
Under the silk of the wrist a sea, tell
Time is nowhere.

We stand; leaves have not timed the
summer.

No clock now needs
Tell we have only what we remember:
Minutes uproaring with our heads

Like an unfortunate King's and his Queen's
When the senseless mob rules;
And quietly the trees casting their crowns
Into the pools.

Love Letter

SYLVIA PLATH

Not easy to state the change you made.
If I'm alive now, then I was dead,
Though, like a stone, unbothered by it,
Staying put according to habit.
You didn't just toe me an inch, no—
Nor leave me to set my small bald eye
Skyward again, without hope, of course,
Of apprehending blueness, or stars.

That wasn't it. I slept, say: a snake
Masked among black rocks as a black
    rock
In the white hiatus of winter—
Like my neighbors, taking no pleasure
In the million perfectly-chiseled
Cheeks alighting each moment to melt
My cheek of basalt. They turned to tears,
Angels weeping over dull natures,
But didn't convince me. Those tears froze.
Each dead head had a visor of ice.

And I slept on like a bent finger.
The first thing I saw was sheer air

And the locked drops rising in a dew
Limpid as spirits. Many stones lay
Dense and expressionless round about.
I didn't know what to make of it.
I shone, mica-scaled, and unfolded
To pour myself out like a fluid
Among bird feet and the stems of plants.
I wasn't fooled. I knew you at once.

Tree and stone glittered, without shadows.
My finger-length grew lucent as glass.
I started to bud like a March twig:
An arm and a leg, an arm, a leg.
From stone to cloud, so I ascended.
Now I resemble a sort of god
Floating through the air in my soul-shift
Pure as a pane of ice. It's a gift.

Marriage Morning

ALFRED, LORD TENNYSON

Traditionally, wedding songs praise the bride or the idea of marriage itself. In this work, the poet praises the morning light on his wedding day, as he races to be wed. Is his heart strong enough for the race, for his tireless love? Clearly the answer is yes.

Light, so low upon earth,
    You send a flash to the sun.
Here is the golden close of love,
    All my wooing is done.
Oh, the woods and the meadows,
    Woods where we hid from the wet,
Stiles where we stay'd to be kind,
    Meadows in which we met!

Light, so low in the vale
    You flash and lighten afar,
For this is the golden morning of love,
    And you are his morning star
Flash, I am coming, I come,
    By meadow and stile and wood,
Oh, lighten into my eyes and heart,
    Into my heart and my blood!

Heart, are you great enough
　For a love that never tires?
O heart, are you great enough for love?
　I have heard of thorns and briers,
Over the meadow and stiles,
　Over the world to the end of it
Flash for a million miles.

To My Dear and Loving Husband

ANNE BRADSTREET

Anne Bradstreet and her husband were married in 1628; they then immigrated to the United States. Her poems were first published in 1650 when a relative surreptitiously took them to England and had them printed—without her knowledge.

If ever two were one, then surely we.
If ever man were loved by wife, then thee;
If ever wife was happy in a man,
Compare with me ye women if you can.
I prize thy love more than whole mines of
　　gold,
Or all the riches that the East doth hold.
My love is such that rivers cannot quench,
Nor ought but love from thee give
　　recompense.
Thy love is such I can no way repay;
The heavens reward thee manifold, I pray.
Then while we live, in love let's so
　　persever,
That when we live no more we may live
　　ever.

Fulfillment

WILLIAM CAVENDISH

William Cavendish understood what is special about love and marriage long before Frank Sinatra sang about it. To this poet, the bonds of matrimony represent the epitome of happiness, a state of endless harmony and unconditional love.

There is no happier life
But in a wife;
The comforts are so sweet
When two do meet.
'Tis plenty, peace, a calm
Like dropping balm;
Love's weather is so fair,
Like perfumed air.
Each word such pleasure brings
Like soft-touched strings;
Love's passion moves the heart
On either part;
Such harmony together,
So pleased in either.
No discords; concords still;
Sealed with one will.
By love, God made man one,

Yet not alone.
Like stamps of king and queen
It may be seen:
Two figures on one coin,
So do they join,
Only they not embrace.
We, face to face.

Theirs was a legendary Victorian romance: the sickly maiden past her youth, the dashingly handsome young poet who carried her off to the Tuscan sunshine, where their love flourished. These poems reflect markedly different perspectives: Hers is a song of praise to their love, and his more an evocation of a passionate encounter.

How Do I Love Thee?

ELIZABETH BARRETT BROWNING

How do I love thee? Let me count the
ways.
I love thee to the depth and breadth and
height
my soul can reach, when feeling out of
sight
For the ends of Being and ideal Grace.
I love thee to the level of every day's
Most quiet need, by sun and candlelight.
I love thee freely, as men strive for Right;
I love thee purely, as they turn from Praise.
I love thee with the passion put to use
In my old griefs, and with my childhood's
faith.
I love thee with a love I seemed to lose

With my lost saints,—I love thee with the breath,
Smiles, tears, of all my life!—and, if God choose,
I shall but love thee better after death.

Meeting at Night

ROBERT BROWNING

The grey sea and the long black land;
And the yellow half-moon large and low;
And the startled little waves that leap
In fiery ringlets from their sleep,
As I gain the cove with pushing prow,
And quench its speed i' the slushy sand.

Then a mile of warm sea-scented beach;
Three fields to cross till a farm appears;
A tap at the pane, the quick sharp scratch
And blue spurt of a lighted match,
And a voice less loud, thro' its joys and
    fears,
Than the two hearts beating each to each!

Sonnet xxx

EDNA ST. VINCENT MILLAY

Millay's poetry is often associated with a sense of passionate abandon. In this brief but pointed work she weighs a romantic sense of the value of passion against more pragmatic concerns, and finds the balance tilts in favor of love.

Love is not all: It is not meat nor drink
Nor slumber nor a roof against the rain;
Nor yet a floating spar to men that sink
And rise and sink and rise and sink again.
Love can not fill the thickened lung with
    breath
Nor clean the blood, nor set the fractured
    bone;
Yet many a man is making friends with death
Even as I speak, for lack of love alone.
It well may be that in a difficult hour,
Pinned down by pain and moaning for
    release,
Or nagged by want past resolution's power,
I might be driven to sell you love for peace,
Or trade the memory of this night for food.
It well may be. I do not think I would.

Camomile Tea

KATHERINE MANSFIELD

Known primarily as a short-story writer, Katherine Mansfield is one of New Zealand's greatest literary figures. Virginia Woolf once said that Mansfield turned out "the only writing I have ever been jealous of." In "Camomile Tea," the pleasures of domestic tranquillity are at once magical and commonplace.

Outside the sky is light with stars;
There's a hollow roaring from the sea.
And, alas! for the little almond flowers,
The wind is shaking the almond tree.

How little I thought, a year ago,
In the horrible cottage upon the Lee
That he and I should be sitting so
And sipping a cup of camomile tea.

Light as feathers the witches fly,
The horn of the moon is plain to see;
By a firefly under a jonquil flower
A goblin toasts a bumble-bee.

We might be fifty, we might be five,
So snug, so compact, so wise are we!
Under the kitchen-table leg
My knee is pressing against his knee.

Our shutters are shut, the fire is low,
The tap is dripping peacefully;
The saucepan shadows on the wall
Are black and round and plain to see.

Enduring love is not the result of a onetime decision; it is making, over and over again, the same choice—the same person. These brief verses have in common an appreciation for a familiar type of love that is born of long-term familiarity and comfort.

Decade

AMY LOWELL

When you came, you were like red wine
and honey,
And the taste of you burnt my mouth with
its sweetness.
Now you are like morning bread,
Smooth and pleasant.
I hardly taste you at all for I know your
savour,
But I am completely nourished.

Wear Me

ROBERT KOGAN

I want you to wear me
comfortably,
as you would a dress,
or the silver necklace that you wear
around your neck.
Comfortably, so that I am always
next to you:
but most important—
something you decide
each morning to select.

The Marriage
YVOR WINTERS

Winters believed that in order for the mind's ear to fully appreciate poetry, poems must be read aloud. This is certainly true in the case of "The Marriage"—reading it aloud produces a range of emotions otherwise unfelt. "The Marriage" is uplifting, sad, and hopeful all at once, analogous to a union that endures ups, downs, and everything in between.

Incarnate for our marriage you appeared,
Flesh living in the spirit and endeared
By minor graces and slow sensual change.
Through every nerve we made our spirits
    range.
We fed our minds on every mortal thing:
The lacy fronds of carrots in the spring,
Their flesh sweet on the tongue, the salty
    wine
From bitter grapes, which gathered
    through the vine
The mineral drouth of autumn concentrate,
Wild spring in dream escaping, the debate
Of flesh and spirit on those vernal nights,

Its resolution in naive delights,
The young kids bleating softly in the rain—
All this to pass, not to return again.
And when I found your flesh did not resist,
It was the living spirit that I kissed,
It was the spirit's change in which I lay:
Thus, mind in mind we waited for the day.
When flesh shall fall away, and, falling,
     stand
Wrinkling with shadow over face and hand,
Still I shall meet you on the verge of dust
And know you as a faithful vestige must.
And, in commemoration of our lust,
May our heirs seal us in a single urn,
A single spirit never to return.

Married Love

TAO-SHENG

This ancient poem is a testament to eternal love. Tao-Sheng describes a love that, like fire, is transformative. The fire of this couple's love forges so complete a union that the two become essentially one, with no boundary between them, in life or in death.

You and I
Have so much love,
That it
Burns like a fire,
In which we bake a lump of clay
Molded into a figure of you
And a figure of me.
Then we take both of them,
And break them into pieces,
And mix the pieces with water,
And mold again a figure of you,
And a figure of me.
I am in your clay.
You are in my clay.
In life we share a single quilt.
In death we will share a single coffin.

The River Merchant's Wife

LI PO

Whether the version of this poem reprinted here owes more to its Chinese creator or its American adaptor is a matter for specialists. What is undeniable is its authentic sentiment of loneliness and longing, an acute awareness of a lover's absence and the passage of time. The translation is by Ezra Pound.

While my hair was still cut straight across
    my forehead
I played about the front gate, pulling
    flowers.
You came by on bamboo stilts, playing
    horse,
You walked about my seat, playing with
    blue plums.
And we went on living in the village of
    Chokan:
Two small people, without dislike or
    suspicion.

At fourteen I married My Lord you.
I never laughed, being bashful.

Lowering my head, I looked at the wall.
Called to, a thousand times, I never looked
    back.

At fifteen I stopped scowling,
I desired my dust to be mingled with yours
Forever and forever, and forever.
Why should I climb the lookout?

At sixteen you departed,
You went into far Ku-to-Yen, by the river of
    swirling eddies,
And you have been gone five months.
The monkeys make sorrowful noise overhead.
You dragged your feet when you went out.
By the gate now, the moss is grown, the
    different mosses,
Too deep to clear them away!
The leaves fall early this autumn, in wind.
The paired butterflies are already yellow
    with August
Over the grass in the West garden,

They hurt me.
I grow older,

If you are coming down through the
    narrows of the river Kiang,
Please let me know beforehand,
And I will come out to meet you,
As far as Cho-fu-Sa.

To His Coy Mistress

ANDREW MARVELL

Marvell's famous poem of seduction is also a meditation on the fragility of human existence and a celebration of the joys of sensual love.

Had we but World enough, and Time,
This coyness lady were no crime.
We would sit down, and think which
   way
To walk, and pass our long love's day;
Thou by the Indian Ganges side
Should'st rubies find: I by the tide
Of *Humber* would complain. I would
Love you ten years before the Flood:
And you should if you please refuse
Till the conversion of the *Jews.*
My vegetable love should grow
Vaster than Empires, and more slow.
An hundred years should go to praise
Thine eyes, and on thy Forehead Gaze;
Two hundred to adore each Breast:
But thirty thousand to the rest;
An age at least to every part,
And the last age should show your heart.

For Lady, you deserve this State;
Nor would I love at lower rate.
    But at my back I always hear
Times winged chariot hurrying near:
And yonder all before us lie
Deserts of vast Eternity.
Thy Beauty shall no more be found,
Nor, in thy marble Vault, shall sound
My echoing song: then Worms shall try
That long preserv'd Virginity:
And your quaint Honour turn to dust;
And into ashes all my Lust.
The Grave's a fine and private place,
But none I think do there embrace.
    Now therefore, while the youthful
      hue
Sits on thy skin like morning dew,
And while thy willing Soul transpires
At every pore with instant Fires,
Now let us sport us while we may;
And now, like am'rous birds of prey,
Rather at once our Time devour,
Than languish in his slow-chapt pow'r.
Let us roll all our Strength, and all
Our sweetness, up into one Ball;

And tear our Pleasures with rough
   strife,
Thorough the Iron gates of Life.
Thus, though we cannot make our Sun
Stand still, yet we will make him run.

Nothing Twice

WISLAWA SZYMBORSKA

Syzmborska, awarded the Nobel Prize for Literature in 1996, displays in her work a direct, pragmatic vision of cosmic events. Here she celebrates her understanding that although life is fundamentally without rules or order, love makes that fact moot. The translation is by Stanislaw Baranczak and Clare Cavanagh.

Nothing can ever happen twice.
In consequence, the sorry fact is
that we arrive here improvised
and leave without the chance to practice.

Even if there is no one dumber,
if you're the planet's biggest dunce,
you can't repeat the class in summer:
this course is only offered once.

No day copies yesterday,
no two nights will teach what bliss is
in precisely the same way,
with exactly the same kisses.

One day, perhaps, some idle tongue
mentions your name by accident:
I feel as if a rose were flung
into the room, all hue and scent.

The next day, though you're here with me,
I can't help looking at the clock:
A rose? A rose? What could that be?
Is it a flower or a rock?

Why do we treat the fleeting day
with so much needless fear and sorrow?
It's in its nature not to stay:
Today is always gone tomorrow.

With smiles and kisses, we prefer to
seek accord beneath our star,
although we're different (we concur)
just as two drops of water are.

Strawberries

EDWIN MORGAN

The different senses sometimes overlap and echo each other. In this poem, the sweet, warm taste and texture of strawberries overflow into a different kind of touching and tasting, and a storm breaking in the heavens mirrors tempestuous union on the earth below.

There were never strawberries
like the ones we had
that sultry afternoon
sitting on the step
of the open french window
facing each other
your knees held in mine
the blue plates in our laps
the strawberries glistening
in the hot sunlight
we dipped them in sugar
looking at each other
not hurrying the feast
for one to come
the empty plates
laid on the stone together

with the two forks crossed
and I bent towards you
sweet in that air
in my arms
abandoned like a child
from your eager mouth
the taste of strawberries
in my memory
lean back again
let me love you
let the sun beat
on our forgetfulness
one hour of all
the heat intense
and summer lightning
on the Kilpatrick hills

let the storm wash the plates

True Love

ROBERT PENN WARREN

Call it a rite of passage, when you suddenly recognize the opposite sex for the first time and new worlds of desire awaken. It's your first love, it's true love. Robert Penn Warren's vividly realized depiction shows us how indelible this first experience can be.

In silence the heart raves. It utters words
Meaningless, that never had
A meaning. I was ten, skinny, red-headed,

Freckled. In a big black Buick,
Driven by a big grown boy, with a necktie,
   she sat
In front of the drugstore, sipping something

Through a straw. There is nothing like
Beauty. It stops your heart. It
Thickens your blood. It stops your breath. It

Makes you feel dirty. You need a hot bath.
I leaned against a telephone pole, and
   watched.
I thought I would die if she saw me.

How could I exist in the same world with
    that brightness?
Two years later she smiled at me. She
Named my name. I thought I would wake
    up dead.

Her grown brothers walked with the bent-
    knee
Swagger of horsemen. They were slick-
    faced.
Told jokes in the barbershop. Did no
    work.

Their father was what is called a
    drunkard.
Whatever he was he stayed on the third
    floor
Of the big white farmhouse under the
    maples for twenty-five years.

He never came down. They brought
    everything up to him.
I did not know what a mortgage was.
His wife was a good, Christian woman,
    and prayed.

When the daughter got married, the old
    man came down wearing
An old tail coat, the pleated shirt yellowing.
The sons propped him. I saw the wedding.
    There were

Engraved invitations, it was so fashionable.
    I thought
I would cry. I lay in bed that night
And wondered if she would cry when
    something was done to her.

The mortgage was foreclosed. That last
    word was whispered.
She never came back. The family
Sort of drifted off. Nobody wears shiny
    boots like that now.

But I know she is beautiful forever, and
    lives
In a beautiful house, far away.
She called my name once. I didn't even
    know she knew it.

When I Was One-and-Twenty

A. E. HOUSMAN

Housman himself apparently lived a rather lonely life, without long-term romantic attachment. Perhaps this explains the poignancy of much of his verse, along with an awareness of the vulnerability that is an unavoidable corollary to unreserved commitment and love.

When I was one-and-twenty
I heard a wise man say,
"Give crowns and pounds and guineas
But not your heart away;
Give pearls away and rubies
But keep your fancy free."
But I was one-and-twenty,
No use to talk to me.

When I was one-and-twenty
I heard him say again,
"The heart out of the bosom
Was never given in vain;
'Tis paid with sighs a plenty
And sold for endless rue."
And I am two-and-twenty
And oh, 'tis true, 'tis true.

Thunderstorm in Town

THOMAS HARDY

Here, reluctance to act results in long-term regret, demonstrating how a botched opportunity in love may haunt a person for a lifetime. For Thomas Hardy, who was known for his pessimism about love (and life in general), this reminiscence is quite mild. (See, in contrast, the fond lifelong remembrance of a brief encounter in the previous poem.)

She wore a "terra-cotta" dress,
And we stayed, because of the pelting
   storm,
Within the hansom's dry recess,
Though the horse had stopped; yea,
   motionless
We sat on, snug and warm.

Then the downpour ceased, to my sharp
   sad pain,
And the glass that had screened our forms
   before
Flew up, and out she sprang to her door:
I should have kissed her if the rain
Had lasted a minute more.

On the Balcony

D. H. LAWRENCE

D. H. Lawrence and his wife, Frieda, had a turbulent marriage. They fought constantly, mostly because their affair—begun when she was married to another man—caused her to lose custody of her children. The poem reflects the struggles they faced and, more important, expresses Lawrence's hope of a better tomorrow where they would still have each other.

In front of the somber mountains,
a faint, lost ribbon of rainbow
And between us and it, the thunder;
And down below in the green wheat,
the laborers stand like dark stumps,
still in the green wheat.
You are near to me, and naked feet
In their sandals, and through the
scent of the balcony's naked timber
I distinguish the scent of your hair:
so now the limber
Lightning falls from heaven.
Adown the pale-green glacier river floats
A dark boat through the gloom—

and whither? The thunder roars
But still we have each other!
The naked lightnings in the heavens dither
And disappear—what have we but each
    other?
The boat has gone.

Love Song

RAINER MARIA RILKE

Rilke's poetry reflects his lifelong melancholy—a condition perhaps deepened by the toll that the complexities of modern life took on his sensitive nature. "Love Song," though among the sweetest of Rilke's poems, still conveys his interpretation of the world as a place where even intimate relationships aren't free of a sense of distance. To the poet the consciousness of this distance may play an essential part in sustaining the mystery of love and life.

How can I keep my soul in me, so that it
doesn't touch your soul?
How can I raise it high enough, past you,
to other things?
I would like to shelter it, among remote lost
objects, in some dark and silent place
that doesn't resonate when your depths
resound.
Yet everything that touches us, me and
you, takes us together like a violin's
bow, which draws one voice out of two
separate strings.

Upon what instrument are we two
spanned?
And what musician holds us in his hand?
Oh sweetest song.

Moonlit Night

TU FU

Generally regarded as the greatest of all Chinese poets, Tu Fu lived a life filled with hardship, which perhaps influenced the humanity and compassion found in his best work. This translation is by the modern Indian poet and novelist Vikram Seth.

In Fuzhou, far away, my wife is watching
The moon alone tonight, and my thoughts
   fill
With sadness for my children, who can't
   think
Of me here in Changan; they're too young
   still.
Her cloud-soft hair is moist with fragrant
   mist.
In the clear light her white arms sense the
   chill.
When will we feel the moonlight dry our
   tears,
Leaning together on our windowsill?

Sonnet of Sweet Complaint

FEDERICO GARCIA LORCA

One of Spain's greatest modern poets, Lorca was brutally killed in 1936 and his work banned by Franco's regime. In this poem, Lorca expresses sadness and fear after the end of a relationship. Yet his hope is that his life will move forward, not despite his lost love, but because of it.

Never let me lose the marvel
of your statue-like eyes, or the accent
the solitary rose of your breath
places on my cheek at night.

I am afraid of being, on this shore,
a branchless trunk, and what I most regret
is having no flower, pulp, or clay
for the worm of my despair.

If you are my hidden treasure,
if you are my cross, my dampened pain,
if I am a dog, and you alone my master,

never let me lose what I have gained,
and adorn the branches of your river
with leaves of my estranged Autumn.

Since There's No Help

MICHAEL DRAYTON

This sonnet by a contemporary of Shake-speare is divided into two parts: In the first a lover seems to cheerfully bid his beloved farewell; but the last six lines indicate that a reconciliation might not, after all, be unwelcome.

Since there's no help, come let us kiss and
    part;
Nay I have done, you get no more of me,
And I am glad, yea, glad with all my heart
That thus so cleanly I myself can free;
Shake hands for ever, cancel all our vows,
And when we meet at any time again,
Be it not seen in either of our brows
That we one jot of former love retain.
Now at the last gasp of Love's latest breath,
When, his pulse failing, Passion speechless
    lies,
When Faith is kneeling by his bed of death,
And Innocence is closing up his eyes,
Now if thou wouldst, when all have given him
    over.
From death to life thou mightst him yet
    recover.

Love Arm'd

APHRA BEHN

Aphra Behn, who lived in seventeenth-century England, was one of the first women known to have made her living by writing. In this allegorical verse she portrays love as an armed tyrant, but one who unfairly harms only her heart, while her lover's triumphs. It's interesting to contrast her use of personification with Michael Drayton's in "Since There's No Help" (previous page).

Love in Fantastique Triumph sat,
Whilst bleeding Hearts around him
   flow'd,
For whom Fresh pains he did create,
And strange Tyranic power he show'd;
From thy Bright Eyes he took his fire,
Which round about, in sport he hurl'd;
But 'twas from mine he took desire,
Enough to undo the Amorous World.
From me he took his sights and tears,
From thee his Pride and Crueltie;
From me his Languishments and
   Feares,
And every Killing Dart from thee;

Thus thou and I, the God have arm'd,
And sett him up a Deity;
But my poor Heart alone is harm'd,
Whilst thine the Victor is, and free.

The Lost Love

WILLIAM WORDSWORTH

*This lovely lyric introduces its subject, Lucy,
as a small, obscure part of the natural world,
but the poem ends with a moving affirmation of her ultimate significance.*

She dwelt among the untrodden ways
Beside the springs of Dove;
A maid whom there were none to praise,
And very few to love:

A violet by a mossy stone
Half hidden from the eye!
Fair as a star, when only one
Is shining in the sky.

She lived unknown, and few could know
When Lucy ceased to be;
But she is in her grave, and oh,
The difference to me!

Echo

CHRISTINA ROSSETTI

Christina Rossetti was the sister of the Pre-Raphaelite painter and poet Dante Gabriel Rossetti, but she was a significant artist in her own right. This poem offers a rhapsodic expression of how a bittersweet memory of past love can at the same time provide vivid recollection of a long-ago passion.

Come to me in the silence of the night;
   Come in the speaking silence of a dream;
Come with soft rounded cheeks and eyes
     as bright
  As sunlight on a stream;
   Come back in tears,
O memory, hope, love of finished years.

O dream how sweet, too sweet, too bitter
    sweet,
  Whose wakening should have been in
    Paradise,
Where souls brimfull of love abide and meet;
  Where thirsting longing eyes
   Watch the slow door
That opening, letting in, lets out no more.

Yet come to me in dreams, that I may live
   My very life again though cold in death:
Come back to me in dreams, that I may
    give
   Pulse for pulse, breath for breath:
    Speak low, lean low,
As long ago, my love, how long ago.

Reminiscence

ANNE BRONTE

Of the three Bronte sisters, the least is known about Anne, the youngest. The first book of theirs published was a collaborative effort written under assumed names. Interestingly, just two copies of this book sold when it was published. Now there is hardly a bookstore that doesn't have many copies of the Brontes' work. Anne, in this sonnet, reflects on the ways her life was graced by the beloved person buried beneath the church floor she paces.

Yes, thou art gone! and never more,
Thy sunny smile shall gladden me;
But I may pass the old church door,
And pace the floor that covers thee.
May stand upon the cold, damp stone,
And think that, frozen, lies below
The lightest heart that I have known,
The kindest I shall ever know.
Yet, though I cannot see thee more,
'Tis still a comfort to have seen;
And though thy transient life is o'er,
'Tis sweet to think that thou hast been;

To think a soul so near divine,
Within a form so angel fair,
United to a heart like thine,
Has gladdened once our humble sphere.

For Jane

CHARLES BUKOWSKI

In his blunt style, Bukowski shows how the death of a lover can cause an anguish ferocious in its power. So profound is his feeling of loss that he becomes oblivious to the grief that surrounds him like tigers.

225 days under grass
and you know more than I.
they have long taken your blood,
you are a dry stick in a basket.
is this how it works?
in this room
the hours of love
still make shadows.

when you left
you took almost
everything.
I kneel in the nights
before tigers
that will not let me be.

what you were
will not happen again.
the tigers have found me
and I do not care.

Funeral Blues

W. H. AUDEN

Few other poems approach the poignancy of this one in its expression of grief at losing a lover. Its economy and colloquial language only serve to heighten the emotional effect. Many will recall this poem being read aloud in the film Four Weddings and a Funeral.

Stop all the clocks, cut off the telephone,
Prevent the dog from barking with a juicy
   bone,
Silence the pianos and with muffled drum
Bring out the coffin, let the mourners come.

Let aeroplanes circle moaning overhead
Scribbling on the sky the message He Is
   Dead,
Put crepe bows round the white necks of
   the public doves,
Let the traffic policemen wear black cotton
   gloves.

He was my North, my South, my East and
   West,
My working week and my Sunday rest,

My noon, my midnight, my talk, my song;
I thought that love would last for ever: I
    was wrong.

The stars are not wanted now: put out
    every one;
Pack up the moon and dismantle the sun;
Pour away the ocean and sweep up the
    wood.
For nothing now can ever come to any
    good.

Vino Tinto

SANDRA CISNEROS

Vividly seductive and earthy, Cisneros's reminiscence is a contemporary narration of sensual love.

Dark wine reminds me of you.
The burgundies and cabernets.
The tang and thrum and hiss
that spiral like Egyptian silk,
blood bit from a lip, black
smoke from a cigarette.

Nights that swell like cork.
This night. A thousand.
Under a single lamplight.
In public or alone.
Very late or very early.
When I write my poems.

Something of you still taut
still tugs still pulls,
a rope that trembled
hummed between us.
Hummed, love, didn't it.
Love, how it hummed.

One Art

ELIZABETH BISHOP

In "One Art," the poet catalogs her losses in such a casual, wry tone as to belie the mounting tension of an escalating tragedy. The poem moves from the triviality of mislaid keys to a disaster so great that in the final line the author must force herself to face it—"(Write it!)"—by putting it on paper.

The art of losing isn't hard to master;
so many things seem filled with the
    intent
to be lost that their loss is no disaster.

Lose something every day. Accept the
    fluster
of lost door keys, the hour badly spent.
The art of losing isn't hard to master.

Then practice losing farther, losing faster:
places, and names, and where it was you
    meant
to travel. None of these will bring
    disaster.

I lost my mother's watch. And look! my
   last, or
next-to-last, of three loved houses went.
The art of losing isn't hard to master.

I lost two cities, lovely ones. And, vaster,
some realms I owned, two rivers, a
   continent.
I miss them, but it wasn't a disaster.

—Even losing you (the joking voice, a
   gesture
I love) I shan't have lied. It's evident
the art of losing's not too hard to master
though it may look like (*Write it!*) like
   disaster.

To Fanny Brawne

JOHN KEATS

Keats was already dying of tuberculosis when he met and then became engaged to Fanny Brawne. The unsentimental yet passionate expression of his sense of imminent loss makes this poem almost unbearably poignant.

This living hand, now warm and capable
Of earnest grasping, would, if it were cold
And in the icy silence of the tomb,
So haunt thy days and chill thy dreaming
    nights
That thou would wish thine own heart dry
    of blood
So in my veins red life might stream again,
And thou be conscience-calmed—see here
    it is—
I hold it toward you.

A Valediction Forbidding Mourning

JOHN DONNE

This is perhaps the highest achievement of this greatest of all the Metaphysical Poets (so-called because of the abstract concepts and intellectualized imagery that characterize their work, often illustrating powerful emotional themes). The central conceit is of two lovers compared to arms of a compass, connected even when apart.

As virtuous men pass mildly away,
And whisper to their souls to go,
Whilst some of their sad friends do say,
Now his breath goes, and some say, No:

So let us melt, and make no noise,
No tear-floods, nor sigh-tempests move,
'Twere profanation of our joys
To tell the laity our love.

Moving of th' earth brings harms and
    fears,
Men reckon what it did, and meant,
But trepidation of the spheres,
Though greater far, is innocent.

Dull sublunary lovers' love
—Whose soul is sense—cannot admit
Of absence, 'cause it doth remove
The thing which elemented it.

But we by a love so much refined,
That ourselves know not what it is,
Inter-assured of the mind,
Care less, eyes, lips and hands to miss.

Our two souls therefore, which are one,
Though I must go, endure not yet
A breach, but an expansion,
Like gold to aery thinness beat.

If they be two, they are two so
As stiff twin compasses are two;
Thy soul, the fix'd foot, makes no show
To move, but doth, if th' other do.

And though it in the center sit,
Yet, when the other far doth roam,
It leans, and hearkens after it,
And grows erect, as that comes home.

Such wilt thou be to me, who must,
Like th' other foot, obliquely run;
Thy firmness makes my circle just,
And makes me end where I begun.

Index to Titles and Authors

(Entries in **boldface** indicate titles)

Alfred, Lord Tennyson, 98–99
Allen, Elizabeth Akers, 52–53
Anonymous, 62
Apollinaire, Guillaume, 18–19
At Last, 52–53
Atwood, Margaret, 93
Auden, W. H., 144–145
Avenue, The, 16
Bargain, The, 17
Baudelaire, Charles, 71–73
Beckett, Samuel, 87
Behn, Aphra, 136–137
Belloc, Hilaire, 37
Between Your Sheets, 69–70
Bishop, Elizabeth, 147–148
Blake, William, 56
Bradstreet, Anne, 100
Brautigan, Richard, 39–40

Bronte, Anne, 141–142
Browning, Elizabeth Barrett, 103–104
Browning, Robert, 105
Bukowski, Charles, 143
Burns, Robert, 9
Byron, Lord, 21
Camomile Tea, 107–108
Catullus (Gaius Valerius Catullus), 74
Cavendish, William, 101–102
Chaucer, Geoffrey, 80
Cisneros, Sandra, 146
Come Quickly, 91
Confession, 78
Cornford, Frances, 16
Cummings, E. E., 14–15
Dante Alighieri, 1
Decade, 109
Dickinson, Emily, 67
Donne, John, 105–152
Drayton, Michael, 135
Echo, 139–140
Enchantment, The, 63
Etherege, Sir George, 84–85
Ewing, Juliana Horatia, 51
Fearing, Kenneth, 33–35
For Jane, 143
Frost, Robert, 64–65
Fulfillment, 101–102
Funeral Blues, 144–145

Gardener, The, 24–25

Gifts, 51

Goethe, Johann Wolfgang von, 23

Graves, Robert, 10

Habitation, 93

Halas, Frantisek, 78

Hall, Donald, 55

Hardy, Thomas, 125

He Is More than a Hero, 81–82

Housman, A. E., 127

How Do I Love Thee?, 103–104

Hughes, Langston, 45

Hughes, Ted, 94–95

Hunt, Leigh, 36

I Carry Your Heart with Me, 14–15

I Do Not Love You, 49–50

I Knew a Woman, 57–59

I Loved You, 79

I Prithee Send Me Back My Heart, 12–13

I Want to Breathe, 89

It Is the Third Watch, 62

Jenny Kiss'd Me, 36

Jewels, The, 71–73

Jimenez, Juan Ramon, 20

Jonson, Ben, 38

Juliet, 37

Keats, John, 149

Kogan, Robert, 110

La Vita Nuova, 1

Lady Love, 87
Last Night You Left Me and Slept, 11
Laughlin, James, 89
Lawrence, D. H., 129–130
Lear, Edward, 41–42
Let Me Not to the Marriage of True Minds, 92
Li Po, 114–116
Lorca, Federico Garcia, 134
Lost Love, The, 138
Love 20 Cents the First Quarter Mile, 33–35
Love Arm'd, 136–137
Love for a Hand, 60–61
Love Letter, 96–97
Love Poem, 88
Love Song to Alex, 1979, 43–44
Love Song (Rilke), 131–132
Love Song (Williams), 66
Love's Secret, 56
Lowell, Amy, 109
Mansfield, Katherine, 107–108
Marlowe, Christopher, 5
Marriage Morning, 98–99
Marriage, The, 111–112
Married Love, 113
Marvell, Andrew, 117–119
Meeting at Night, 105
Merciless Beauty, 80
Millay, Edna St. Vincent, 106

Milton, John, 6–7
Mirabeau Bridge, The, 18–19
Montagu, Lady Mary Wortley, 69–70
Moonlit Night, 133
Morgan, Edwin, 122–123
Moss, Howard, 4
Nash, Ogden, 47
Neruda, Pablo, 49–50
Night Thoughts, 23
Nothing Twice, 120–121
O'Hara, Frank, 26–27
On the Balcony, 129–130
One Art, 147–148
One Word Is Too Often Profaned, 48
Orr, Gregory, 88
Otway, Thomas, 63
Owl and the Pussy-Cat, The, 41–42
Paradise Lost (Book IV), 6–7
Paz, Octavio, 86
Plath, Sylvia, 96–97
Poe, Edgar Allan, 8
Pushkin, Alexander Sergeyevich, 79
Ragged Wood, The, 22
Red, Red Rose, A, 9
Reminiscence, 141–142
Reprise, 47
Rilke, Rainer Maria, 131–132
River Merchant's Wife, The, 114–116
Roethke, Theodore, 57–59

Rossetti, Christina, 139–140
Rumi, 11
Sappho, 81–82
September, 94–95
Shakespeare, William, 2–3, 92
Shall I Compare Thee to a Summer's Day? (Moss) 4
Shall I Compare Thee to a Summer's Day? (Shakespeare) 2–3
Shapiro, Karl, 60–61
She Comes Not When Noon Is on the Roses, 68
She Tells Her Love while Half Asleep, 10
She Walks in Beauty, 21
Shelley, Percy Bysshe, 48
Shikibu, Izumi, 91
Sidney, Sir Philip, 17
Silken Tent, The, 64–65
Since There's No Help, 135
Solomon, King, 76–77
Song 5 to Lesbia, 74
Song of Songs, The, 76–77
Song to Celia, 38
Sonnet of Sweet Complaint, 134
Sonnet XXX, 106
Statue of Eros, A, 90
Stein, Gertrude, 54
Strawberries, 122–123
Suckling, Sir John, 12–13

Szymborska, Wislawa, 120–121
Tagore, Rabindranath, 24–25
Tao-Sheng, 113
Teasdale, Sara, 46
Thomson, James, 75
Those Who Love, 46
Thunderstorm in Town, 128
To a Stranger, 28–29
To Alice B. Toklas, 54
To Fanny Brawne, 149
To Helen, 8
To His Coy Mistress, 117–119
To His Mistress, 83
To Little or No Purpose, 84–85
To My Dear and Loving Husband, 100
To the Bridge of Love, 20
To the Harbormaster, 26–27
Touch, 86
Trench, Herbert, 68
True Love (Viorst), 30–32
True Love (Warren), 124–126
Tu Fu, 133
Valediction Forbidding Mourning, A,
   150–152
Valentine, 55
Vine, The, 75
Vino Tinto, 146
Viorst, Judith, 30–32
Walker, Margaret, 43–44

Warren, Robert Penn, 124–126
Wear Me, 110
When I Was One-and-Twenty, 127
When Sue Wears Red, 45
Whitman, Walt, 28–29
Who Ever Loved, 5
Wild Nights! 67
Williams, William Carlos, 66
Wilmot, John, Earl of Rochester, 83
Winters, Yvor, 111–112
Wordsworth, William, 138
Yeats, William Butler, 22
Your Catfish Friend, 39–40
Zenodotos, 90

Index to First Lines

"225 days under grass," 143

"A black biplane crashes through the
window," 88

"All right. I may have lied to you and about
you," 33–35

"As virtuous men pass mildly away," 150–152

"At last, when all the summer shine," 52–53

"Between your sheets you soundly sleep,"
69–70

"Chipmunks jump, and greensnakes slither," 55

"Come and let us live my Deare," 74

"Come quickly," 91

"Come to me in the silence of the night,"
139–140

"Dark wine reminds me of you," 146

"Do you really think I would yes I would," 54

"Drink to me, only, with thine eyes," 38

"Geniuses of countless nations," 47

"Had we but World enough, and Time,"
117–119

161

"He is a god in my eyes," 81–82

"Helen, thy beauty is to me," 8

"How can I keep my soul in me, so that it doesn't touch your soul," 131–132

"How did the party go in Portman Square?" 37

"How do I love thee? Let me count the ways," 103–104

"I am the rose of Sharon, and the lily of the valleys," 76–77

"i carry your heart with me," 14–15

"I did but look and love a while," 63

"I do not love you as if you were salt-rose, or topaz," 49–50

"I knew a woman, lovely in her bones," 57–59

"I lie here thinking of you," 66

"I loved you, and I probably still do," 79

"I prithee send me back my heart," 12–13

"I want to breathe," 89

"I want you to wear me comfortably," 110

"I wanted to be sure to reach you," 26–27

"If ever two were one, then surely we," 100

"If I were to live my life," 39–40

"In front of the somber mountains," 129–130

"In Fuzhou, far away, my wife is watching," 133

"In silence the heart raves. It utters words," 124–126

"In that book which is my memory," 1

"Incarnate for our marriage you appeared," 111–112
"It is the third watch," 62
"It is true love because," 30–32
"It lies not in our power to love or hate," 5
"Jenny kiss'd me when we met," 36
"Last night you left me and slept," 11
"Let me not to the marriage of true minds," 92
"Light, so low upon earth," 98–99
"Love in Fantastique Triumph sat," 136–137
"Love is not all: It is not meat nor drink," 106
"Marriage is not a house or even a tent," 93
"My hands open the curtains of your being," 86
"My monkey-wrench man is my sweet patootie," 43–44
"My true love hath my heart, and I have his," 17
"My well-beloved was stripped," 71–73
"Never let me lose the marvel," 134
"Never seek to tell thy love," 56
"Not easy to state the change you made," 96–97
"Nothing can ever happen twice," 120–121
"O my luve's like a red, red rose," 9
"O, hurry, where by water, among the trees," 22
"One word is too often profaned," 48
"Outside the sky is light with stars," 107–108

163

"Passing stranger! you do not know," 28–29

"Shall I compare thee to a Summer's Day?" 2–3

"She comes not when Noon is on the roses," 68

"She dwelt among the untrodden ways," 138

"She is as in a field a silken tent," 64–65

"She is standing on my lids," 87

"She tells her love while half asleep," 10

"She walks in beauty, like the night," 21

"She wore a 'terra-cotta' dress," 128

"Since there's no help, come let us kiss and part," 135

"Stars, you are unfortunate, I pity you," 23

"Stop all the clocks, cut off the telephone," 144–145

"The art of losing isn't hard to master," 147–148

"The grey sea and the long black land," 105

"The Owl and the Pussy-cat went to sea," 41–42

"The wine of Love is music," 75

"There is no happier life but in a wife," 101–102

"There were never strawberries like the ones we had," 122–123

"This living hand, now warm and capable," 149

"Those who love the most," 46

"To little or no purpose I spent many days,"
   84–85

"To the bridge of love," 20

"Touched by all that love is," 78

"Two hands lie still, the hairy and the white,"
   60–61

"Under the Mirabeau bridge the Seine," 18–19

"We sit late, watching the dark slowly unfold,"
   94–95

"When I was one-and-twenty," 127

"When Susanna Jones wears red," 45

"When you came, you were like red wine and
   honey," 109

"While my hair was still cut straight across my
   forehead," 114–116

"Who carved Love," 90

"Who has not seen their lover," 16

"Who says you're like one of the dog days?"
   4

"Why dost thou shade thy lovely face?" 83

"Wild nights! Wild nights!" 67

"With thee conversing I forget all time," 6–7

"Yes, thou art gone! and never more,"
   141–142

"You and I have so much love," 113

"You ask me what since we must part," 51

"Your eyen two will slay me suddenly," 80

"Your questioning eyes are sad," 24–25

Acknowledgments

"He Is More Than a Hero" by Sappho from *Sappho: A New Translation*, translated by Mary Bernard. Copyright © 1958 by the Regents of the University of California, renewed 1986 by Mary Bernard.

"To the Bridge of Love" by Juan Ramon Jimenez and translated by James Wright, reprinted by permission of Wesleyan University Press.

"The Mirabeau Bridge" from *Alcools: Poems by Guillaume Apollinaire*, English translations. Copyright © 1995 by Donald Revell and reprinted by permission of Wesleyan University Press.

"The River Merchant's Wife: A Letter" by Ezra Pound, from *Personae,* copyright ©